THE BLUE

AND

THE GRAY

POEMS

JOSHUA NORTON

Cherry Valley Editions

Publication of this book has been made possible
by a grant from the Coordinating Council of
Literary Magazines which it has made through
funds received from the New York State Council
on the Arts.

This project is supported by
a grant from the N.E.A. in
Washington, D.C., a federal
agency.

"A Fibonacci Book."

cover collage by Paul Grillo

photo by Jackie Doctrow

Library of Congress Cataloging in Publication Data

Norton, Joshua J   1946-
    The Blue and the Gray.

    I. Title.
PS3564.O77B6   811'.5'4   75-33960
ISBN 0-916156-09-5

For

    Charles Plymell
    neon of blue

    Henry Taylor
    horse show of gray

    Elliott Coleman
    color of both

    Thank you.

THE BLUE

Introduction

THE GRAY

Introduction

THE BLUE

once redeemed
now revealed
Climate tones Custom
Sews the Sea
Weaned
Curls the Color
Voice
Blue.

HAMPTON

Seven miles
Inland
Still
The change
Climate
Spices
Exeter
East
Nine miles
Seaward
Stir
The change
Current
Salts
Portsmouth
The center
Seats
Hampton...

Lafayette
Toll road
Highway
The Lane home

Bright
Shuttered
Shadow
Blurred
Building
Decayed
Pine
Devised
Pane
Toby's Drug...

Entrance
The Depot
Train
Boston & Maine
Rusted
Cycle
Honda
Racy...

Carriage shop
Buggy
Modeled
Assembly line
Horseless
Lamie's Tavern

Run
Rum
Tinged
Tonic
Grave yard
Stones
Moss slate
Weathered
Silver marble...

Blue miles
Skybound
Stain
The change
Color
Shades
North.

THE PREP SCHOOL

Providence
Quaker
Prepped
Tweed
Tie
Looped
Quiz
Line
Taught
Butt
Bull
Pressured
Master
Mercy
The C.

RED TIDE

The Red Tide
Returns
Sun drenched shores
And
Blue skies
Flows high
Bringing. . .not merely
A thick tang
Contained in
And
Distributed by
A gas
Known only
Amoeba agent
. . . but a sick sleep
Shown wholly
Scattered
String still
Hollow-eyed
Bite-ragged
Fish
Bodies glisten

Noon
And
Midnight
Rays
And line
The now
Soiled sands
Bleached beaches
            dotted
            adulterated
Red fern-like weed...

Where
The seed
Neptune's cancer
            conceived
                        fused
                            and delivered

Dazzles all

But
Father of Olympus
Mystery
Hawaii's Breadfruit Tree
Dazzled adventurers
        Botany
        believers. . .

Yet
Cycle
Systematic
Tide
Turned.

THE RIDING FARM

North
Country
Corralled
Dirt
Driveway
Worn
Wing
Draped
Limbs
Elm
Entry
Barn
Lathered
Sweat
Hay
Salted
Horse
Saddled
Trailrides & Lessons
Taught
Time
Harnessed
Hooper's Stable...

Elm
Dutch
Disease
Dude
Ranch
Ridden
Dandy
Spurred
Steed
Sway
Back
Run
Spirit
Splintered
Stalls
Bridle
Slack
Stirrup
Blister
Roped
Boredom
Brand
Singed
Shady Acres...

Barn
Breath
Rolled
Clean
Ring
Trainer
Curried
Thoroughbred
Seated
Equitation & English
Show
September Farm.

THE BROWN HOME

Hampton
Holding
High Street
Rut
Riddled
Cart
Rolled
Cobble
Paved
Pitch
Patroned
Caretakers
Catered
Plumbers
Puddled
Tradition
Inspired
Trade
Tooled
Inheritance
The Brown Home...

Puritan
Nourished
Precedent

Rendered
Respect
Half
Split
Generation
Feud
Partition...

Neatness
Needle
Threaded
Shingle
Sound
Plaster
Paint
Trimmed
Garden
Grain...

Squalor
Scent
Thickened
Beam
Break
Window
Waste

Tracked
Garbage
Gravel...

View
Consumed
Self
Conceived.

PLAY STAGE

Saturday
Shrank
September
Past
Eternity
Extended
Weather
Wrapped
Undershirt & Sweater
Unfolded
Stage & Show
Linked
Day
Make-shift
Blueprint
Street & Block
Main-line
Suburb
Stream & Breeze
Limbo
Childhood
Danced...

Performance
Squirrel
Dead
Fluid
Vapor
Lit
Lighter
Flame
Kindled
Curled
Smoke
Vision
Placed
Puzzle (yellow line)
Play
Cremation...

Curtain
Drawn.

GILLY'S WAGON

Portsmouth
The town
Fishing
Built
Boats
Mackerel and Cod
Netted
Traps
Lobster
Baited
Submarine
Base
Submerged
Swims
The past
Blown
Northeaster
Pleasant
The street
Bike shop
Gallagher's
Bank
N.H. saving . . .

Gilly's Wagon
Wood
Horse
Pulled 1900
Beans and Stew
Chowder
Chatter
Needlers & Netters
Sailmakers & Sailors
Catch
The clatter
Metal
Truck
Propelled 1960
Dogs and Burgers
Bean
Babble
Drunks & Drifters
Hippies & Hipsters
Beat
The concert...

Gilly's cry
The same
Six days
Daily

6 P.M. to 6 A.M.
365
Traffic
Tickets
Parked
Illegal
Token
Five dollar
Carnival
Unbroken.

THE DUMP

Farm
Old
Road
Fashioned
Routine
Weather
Whirled
Blue
Washed
Seasons
Waxed and Waned
Annual
Aged
Green
Riveted
Pick-up
Sparked
'48 G.M.C.
Painted
Running board & Side board
Squeaked
Task
Rattled
Trip...

Scenic
Route
Dairy
Milked
Daybreak
Culture
Liberated
Library
Read
School
Recessed
Court
Ruled
Town
Steepled
Church
Sociable
Choired
Country
Tree
Traced
Apple & Acorn
Field
Fodder
Fetched
Tractor
Aided

Minute
Mowed
Mile
Wind
Whisked
Arrival
The Dump...

Dung
Draped
Shrubs
Screened
Damage
Shack
Disclosed
Sign
Shooting & Hunting
Prohibited
Targets
Produced
Rat
Refuge
Thrived
Trash
Reared
Pollution
Pampered

Crows
Clamored
Scavenger
Tongue
Selected
Scraps
Rationed
Can
Contained
Recipe...

Crop
Rind
Fruit
Rot
Festered
Canker
Garden
Seed
Vegetable
Spit
Vomited
Germ
Worm
Flavored
Weeds

Varied
Wrapper...

Smoke
Skirt
Fumed
Fabric
Fire
Smoldered
Swamp
Colored
China
Castoff
Clock
Cuckoo
Cradled
Tick
Buried
Bite
Snake
Coiled
Tub
Bath
Stench
Trickled
Shower

Curtain
Grime
Ground
Crib
Casket
Crusted
Open
Jars
Oozed
Jam
Mold
Collected
Magazines
Comic
Flown
Fly
Classic.

THE GRAY

once renounced
now remembered
Time softens Temper
Laces the Land
Virgin
Coils the Color
Wed
Gray.

JOSH THOMAS

Lee Highway
Seasoned
Fresh gray
By way
Frank's
            A.B.C.
                    On and off
A South will rise
Ran
Curdled
Uncleaned
            tap
                lines
Cracked
        pool
                cues
Shenandoah cut-out
A road by both colors even now forgotten
Mosby's Rangers
Prime
Surrendered
Tinker Mountain...

Leaves
Wove
Calico patterns
Sky
As breath
Cold
Smoked
The puff
Hot
A chimney cabin
        baked mud
        together held
        stones
        stolen walls
Logs limbs fallen
        pegged hand hewn
        crack filled
        twigs
        tapped sap
Roof tar paper...

Remains
Hung-over
Came
The sound
            a "twelve-string"
            now "eight"
The song
Josh Thomas
Sang
      (learned him
       a cotton coon)
Cracked voice
                "Leadbelly" style
                tuned "Doc Watson"
"Fore I die
Four more things
I want to ride
                a ferris wheel
                a fast train
                a bow-legged woman
                and an automobile
Fore I die. . ."

VISTA VOLUNTEER

Love child
Flowered
Chairman
Board of Revlon
Make-up
New York
City-rich
Rocked
Lead guitar
Recorded
Folk
East Village
Poetry
Flew
Jet
South to Roanoke
Exited
Hippies and Heroin
Echoed
History
The road
Volvo wagon
Step right in...

The Draft
        Canada
Vista...

Long way
Eighth Avenue
Subway
Stop
Carbon Kentucky
        blue grass
Strained blown
        coal mines
Stripped cold
        black man
Stained blank...

Out house
One room
Sweated
Salty and Sour
Stuffed
Mattress
Bed bugs
Eating
A hundred years
Bigot bite
Bad itch
Mixed skin...

Ring
Telephone
Scare
"Vista man
Don't want
You
Federal people
Here
Can handle
Our own
Kind"
Click.

GRACE FREEMAN

Tinker Mountain
Flakes
Dusted
"Because it is there"
As time
Rang
Clear
The steel
Muffled
A wood cherry-dog slat
                    banged rusty
                    formed jigsaw
                    nails
                    nicked hardware
Hinged
Josh Thomas
Gray blind
            "fat woman
            come on the run
            your fat legs
            got me on the sun..."

Baled straw
Rocked
Grace Freeman
        cocaine
        round the brain
        head piece
        Hattie Mcdaniels
Boiled belly
        salt pork
        hot stuff
        potato soup
        pigeon cured
Ice cream vanilla specially with gravy
Hummed
Kitchen kettles
        "I'll never marry
        a railroad man
        the reason I'll tell you why
        I never met
        a railroad man
        that wouldn't tell his wife a lie
That wouldn't tell his wife a lie..."

THE SHOOTING STAR

The guard rail
Locked forward
Stomachs
Lurched back
Heads
The seat
And the car
A hundred souls
Moved upward
Catching
Skipped beats
The coaster's heart
Rushed
Forgotten wind
The body's pulse
Faces
Mirrored
The fair grounds
Antediluvian kingdom
Sliding glass
Rounded
The first curve
Broke the gravity
Suspended animation
Dropped the horizon
Rocketed...

Salem U.S.A.
Main street
Virginia
Carry me back
Plantation mansions
Vined 17th
House Of The Seven Gables
Pillared 20th
Gone With The Wind
A Century
War between the States
Cemetery
Fostered
Lotz Funeral Parlor
Cremated
Harvest Ford
Stock car king
The race track wrecks
Fired
Kayo gas
Cooked
Lendy's
The "Buddy Boy..."

Rhythmic beats
Flowed
The last curve
Renewed calm
Sustained the gravity
Grounded animation
Leveled the horizon
The sixty-second ride...

"The Shooting Star
America's highest
World's fastest."

KEYSTONE

Three hours
West of Roanoke
On the
Virginia
West Virginia
Line
Where
Sad deserted
color the sky
Where
Cuckoos calling
sound the air
Where
Buckeye and Sycamore
smell the land
Where
Invisible poor
vision the life...

Headstone
Haunts
The town
Keystone

Where
Bad times
And
Big machines
Said
Farewell
To the
U.M.W. of A.
The pay
Tattoo
Blue coal
And
Cool slate
Needle
Rumble
And
Dark
The mine...

Now
Rubber tires
Whine
And
Say
Hello
To the
Row road

Now
Red the color
shot the sound
Now
Gun the tool
whiskey the smell
Forsaken the visible
undone the death.

JOSH AND GRACE

Drops
Soaked
Gray brick road
As sight
Dyed
Tears
The memory
Smiles
A fiber fair-to-middlin
        picked finger measured
        gin separated
        seeds
        sowed cotton
Cloaked
Josh and Grace
A South had risen
        "take a load off fanny
        take a load off brain
        baby keep the faith
        maybe it'll rain
Baby keep the faith…"

THE DELTA

Black
And
Flat
The Delta
Runs
From the
Lobby
Hotel Peabody
Memphis
To the
Loop
Catfish Row
Vicksburg
And
Sustains
Starving
Sharecroppers
Souls
Sold
Whitetrash
And
Boy

Owned
By the
Man
And the
Big white house...

The wage
Squeezed
Shiftless
Soy beans
And
Cotton
Crop percent
Composed
Shanties
Dog trot
And
Cinder block
Four room...

Slavery
Saving
Existence
Not
Admitted
Exhaustion

No. 3 can limas
Grits
Cheap margarine
And
Debt...

Polluted
And
Pregnant
Position
Runs
The Delta.

THE WATERMELON MAN

Ummmm. . .
Whirrrr. . .
Clutch
Shifted
Third
Season
Geared
Heat
Gray
Wound
Whirlwinds
Dust
Stirred
Feather
Hover
Plucked
Chickens
Mowed
Down
Red
Marked
Chevy
'58 third-hand
Plated

Clay
Dirt
Hooded
Road...

Sun
Siesta
Slowed
Coupe
Cough
Choked
Trance
Suspended
Sign
Finger-painted
Polka-dots
Framed
Stand
Carton
Color
Patched
Tree
Peach
Wood
Shaped
Sam
The Watermelon Man...

History
Weathered
Stature
Haggard
Hair
Soot
Whitened
Beard
Salt & Pepper
Pitted
Skin
Bark
Scraped
Pulse
Beat
Pierced
Ear
Egg
Shattered
Eye
Ember...

Earth
Worn
Cloth
Wrinkle
Clung

Body
Bulge
"watermelon
fifty-cent"
Coated
Soul
Soft
"eat one
won't repent"
"one-fifty"
More
"best watermelon. . ."

Hands
Oozed
Sweat
Bottle
Opened
"TomTalor"
Stilled
Heritage
Ink
Blotched
The make. . .

Content
Poured
Un-plugged
Pocket
Re-plugged
Mix
Melon
Placed
Left-over
Trough
Covered
Fountain
Glass
Cracked
Glaze
Seal
Frozen
Sun
Touch
Blazed
Moist
Blade
Flashed
Machete
Eighteen inch
Fell

Wedges
Eight
"best watermelon. . ."

Ummmm. . .
Whirrrr. . .
Clutch
Shifted
Third
Geared
Thought
Watermelon Man.

CHERRY VALLEY EDITIONS
Box 303,
Cherry Valley,
New York 13320